Thinking of You

A TREASURY OF HANDMADE CARDS

We all do it. And it's only human. Whether it's antique ironstone or MP3 files, we all accumulate objects that connect us to the past, to each other or to what we just can't live without. We collect things that are valuable, we keep things that are meaningful and we display things that are beautiful. All those qualities and virtues are inherent in the handcrafted cards you'll find throughout the pages of this book. Create and send one today. You'll not only be thinking of the special people in your life, you'll also be showing them just how important they are. May all the cards be inspiring to create and rewarding to give.

Contents

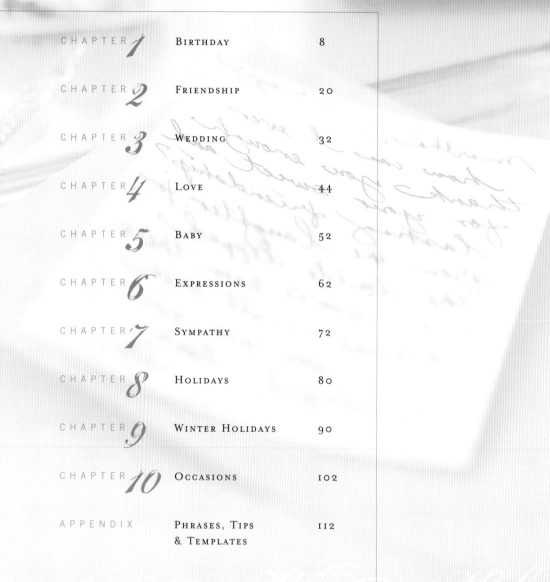

Thinking of You
Love Wedding Friendship
ssions Sympathy Occasions

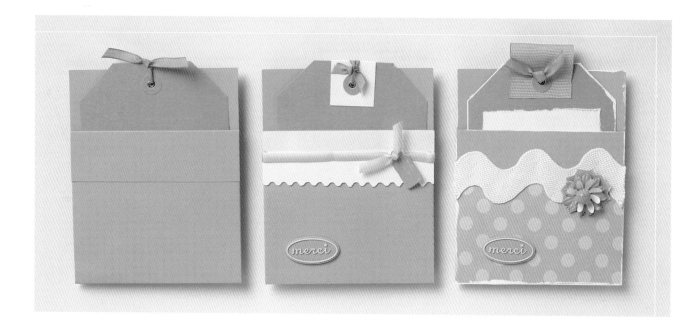

Building a beautiful card is a little like building a beautiful house.

Everything starts with a good, solid foundation. Once that's in place,

you add daring details and tasteful touches to make it all your own.

Using this philosophy, Making Memories® has developed an exclusive

Card Program that makes creating one-of-a-kind cards easier than ever.

With a full line of styles, colors and sizes of cards and embellishments,

you'll start constructing cherished greetings and stop measuring, cutting

and fussing. Throughout this book, you'll be introduced to just a few of

the ways these cards can be used. Then it's all up to you. So make them

simple or make them intricate-just make them beautiful.

Birthday

Card · Party ·

CHAPTER 1

Another Year Older

Celebrating Life

Surprise!

Turning Nine

turning nine · turning ninety · giving a party · going to a party · sweet sixteen · over the hill · growing up · growing old · celebrating life · surprise! · remembering birth · eating cake · blowing out candles · want all his wishes to come true · another year older · passing of time · because it only comes once a year · topping a present · sharing the day

Make every birthday an occasion to remember.

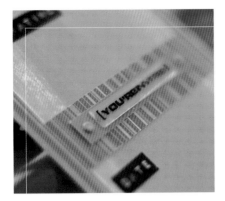

YOU'RE INVITED
by erin terrell

INVITATION
Blossom, coastline embellishment paper, jelly label, mini brads and snap: Making Memories
Label maker: DYMO

HOW TO: Use a Making Memories upright slot card as a template for creating a card and insert out of patterned paper and cardstock. Sand the insert and slide into slot. Cut one wide strip and one thin strip of coordinating cardstock. Add a Blossom to the top edge of the wide strip and secure with a snap in the center. Adhere the thin strip in the middle of the slot, add mini brads to each end and place Jelly Label in the center. Print text with label maker and attach along left side. TIME: 15 MINUTES

RESERVED FOR
by erin terrell

PLACE CARD
Blossom, coastline embellishment paper and mini brad: Making Memories
Label maker: DYMO

HOW TO: Cut a 4½ x 3½-inch piece of striped paper and fold in half. Unfold, lay flat and cut two slits on either side of front flap starting ½ inch in from the edges. Cut a piece of coordinating cardstock so that it will slide through slits and slightly overhang the edges of the card. Lightly sand strip and insert. Secure a Blossom in the bottom right corner with a mini brad, print title on label maker and adhere.

TIME: 5 MINUTES

THANKS
by erin terrell

THANK YOU CARD
Blossom, coastline embellishment paper, eyelet, jump ring, ribbon, rub-ons mini, snap and tag: Making Memories
Label maker: DYMO

HOW TO: Cut double-sided patterned paper to 6 x 12 inches and fold to create card. Cut a 1¾-inch square in the front flap of the card ¾ inch down from the fold. Trim coordinating paper to 5¾-inch square and cut a 2-inch square in the center ½ inch down from the top edge. Lightly sand and adhere to front flap. Windows should line up. Attach Blossom inside with a snap. Cut a 12 x 1½-inch strip of patterned paper, wrap it around the front flap and secure inside. Add a thin strip of solid paper over wide strip and tie ribbon on top. Apply rub-on to a vellum tag, set an eyelet in the hole and dangle from ribbon using a jump ring. Print text with label maker and attach. TIME: 15 MINUTES

Birthday Party Set

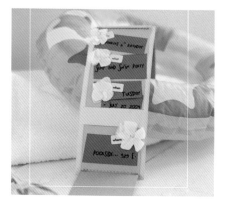

POOL SHACK
by jennifer jensen

INVITATION
Adhesive: Mod Podge by Plaid
Cardstock, cardstock tags, jelly label, mini brads, scrapbook colors acrylic paint, tag and upright slot card base and card: Making Memories
Other: Decorative tag, raffia and tissue paper

HOW TO: Cut two strips of cardstock measuring 3¼ x 6¾ and 3¼ x 4 inches. Line up edges of strips to short ends of insert and zigzag stitch together to create two hinged flaps. Cut clusters of raffia, place inside longer flap and stitch to secure. Adhere decorative tag to oval tag and brush Mod Podge over the top. Paint three stripes on the top flap, let dry, sand lightly and attach Jelly Label. Print party information on cardstock, cut and attach to insert. Cut or punch flower shapes from four layers of tissue paper and secure next to text blocks with mini brads. Adhere cardstock tags to party information, lightly edge insert and card with paint and slide insert through slot.

TIME: 25 MINUTES

SURFBOARD
by jennifer jensen

PLACE CARD (template included)
Foam stamp, hinge, mini brad and scrapbook colors acrylic paint: Making Memories
Other: Balsa wood, tissue paper

HOW TO: Cut surfboard shape out of thin balsa wood using scissors. Cut the bottom half of shape again as well as a small fin for the back. Paint a thin base coat to all pieces and when dry, add stripes to the front. Lightly sand to give the appearance of a well-used board. Glue a hinge to the top of the bottom half piece and attach to the back of the surfboard to create a standing place card. Stamp initial of party guest on the front, cut or punch a flower shape from four layers of tissue and secure with a mini brad. Glue flower just below initial and attach fin to back to complete.

TIME: 15 MINUTES

THANKS
by jennifer jensen

THANK YOU CARD
Cardstock, eyelet, mini brads, rub-ons mini and scrapbook colors acrylic paint: Making Memories
Other: Balsa wood, raffia

HOW TO: Cut cardstock to 4¼ x 8½ inches. Fold bottom up 2¾ inches and stitch around edges to create a pocket. Cut and sand a square of complementary patterned cardstock and attach to flap of pocket. Paint a small square of balsa wood and when dry, lightly sand and apply rub-on. Poke holes into either side of wood and embellish with mini brads. Glue to top of cardstock square on flap. Print a note directly onto a photo from the party, set an eyelet in the upper corner, tie raffia through and slip into pocket.

TIME: 20 MINUTES

43

by julie turner

CARD

Alphabet rub-ons, eyelets, leather label holder, mini brads, rub-ons, scrapbook dye, snaps, staples, tag, upright window card base and woven label: Making Memories
Computer font: Palatino by WordPerfect
Fusible web: Heat 'n' Bond by Therm-o-Web
Ribbon: Mokuba
Other: Fabric, transparency

HOW TO: Use fusible web to adhere striped fabric to front of card. Trim the edges and cut out square opening. Run the card through a printer to add the words to the Happy Birthday song or other greeting. Splatter a coordinating color of dye on a piece of white fabric and, when dry, use fusible web to adhere it to the inside of the card. Use snaps and a staple to attach pieces of cotton ribbon across the square opening. Secure where the ribbons cross with an eyelet. Set eyelets down the right side of the card and lace with ribbon. Dye a scrap of paper and add the number of the birthday using alphabet rub-ons. Staple to the front of the card and attach a Woven Label to the bottom left corner.

Inside the card, layer a gift card and a dyed tag for a handwritten greeting. Apply rub-ons to a piece of transparency film, place behind a Leather Label Holder and attach over the layered pieces. TIME: 60 MINUTES

ENVELOPE

Envelope: Silver Crow
Mini brads and scrapbook dye: Making Memories
Ribbon: Mokuba
Other: Fabric

HOW TO: Dip the envelope flap in dye that matches card. Adhere fabric to cardstock and cut out two circles. Attach to envelope with brads and add ribbon to create a decorative closure.

TIME: 10 MINUTES

15

BIRTHDAY GIFT CARD POCKET
by mellette berezoski

Coastline embellishment paper, hinge, jelly label, label holder
and ribbon: Making Memories
Paper: Bazzill and Scrapbook Wizard
Pocket template: Deluxe Designs
Other: Vellum

HOW TO: Cut a piece of black cardstock to 5½ x 8½ inches
and fold in half. Cut a piece of striped paper to 4 x 5¼
inches. Trim floral paper to 3¼ x 5¼ inches and attach to
right side of striped paper. Attach ribbon where edges of
paper meet to cover seam and wrap around to the back. Add
an open hinge to upper left side to embellish. Use template
to create a pocket out of vellum, attach at an angle on front
of card and slide in gift card. Place Jelly Label behind a label
holder, adhere and secure with ribbon looped through
holes and wrapped around the back. Add corner made of
coordinating cardstock to upper right corner and attach
entire embellished block to front of black card. Place a
piece of white cardstock trimmed to 4 x 5¼ inches inside
for a place to include written greeting. TIME: 35 MINUTES

BIRTHDAY WISHES
by robin johnson

Classic small card base, cardstock tags, jump ring, mini brads, patterned card-
stock, ribbon and woven labels: Making Memories
Decorative scissors: Fiskars
Embroidery floss: DMC

HOW TO: Place Woven Label on cardstock that matches card
and trim so that edges are slightly larger than label. Mat
again with cardstock and trim. Back stitch with embroidery
floss around the edge of the label and first cardstock mat.
Cut a 2-inch strip of patterned cardstock to the width of
the card. Cut the bottom edge with decorative scissors and
mat with cardstock. Punch a small hole in the bottom right
side and hang two embellished tags from a jump ring.
Adhere pieces together. Finish by adding flower mini brads
and ribbon. Attach entire block to front of card.

TIME: 20 MINUTES

YOU'RE INVITED
by loni stevens

Charmed plaque mini, eyelet, eyelet letter, gatefold card base and insert, jump ring, metal word, oversized page pebble, scrapbook colors acrylic paint and stitched tin tile: Making Memories
Computer fonts: Avant Garde by Microsoft Word, CBX Armymen by Chatterbox, CK Newsprint by Creating Keepsakes and Hootie downloaded from the Internet
Ribbon: Li'l Davis Designs
Sticker: Pebbles Inc.

HOW TO: Paint Eyelet Letter number and metal word using acrylic paint. Rub matching paint into Charmed Plaque Mini, wipe away excess and set all pieces aside to dry. Trim insert to a 4½-inch square. Cut a matching piece of cardstock to 9 x 4½ inches and fold in half. Print greeting on front flap of folded piece using coordinating colors. Print invitation information on the trimmed insert using same font colors. Place insert inside folded piece and stitch along inside middle edge to create a small book. Position a large square sticker in the center below title on the front flap and place an oversized Page Pebble over the top. Clip the edge off a Stitched Tin Tile and attach to the center right edge of cover. Punch a hole in the middle and set a ¾-inch eyelet in the center. Dangle the painted number from a jump ring and tie a strip of ribbon through the eyelet. Inside, attach painted metal word to left flap and painted plaque to bottom right corner. TIME: 30 MINUTES

CELEBRATE
by lynne montgomery

Charmed word, classic small card base, eyelets, leather flowers, ledger paper, mini brads, ribbon, staples and tag: Making Memories
Computer font: Times New Roman by Microsoft Word
Paper: KI Memories
Stamping ink: Ranger Industries
Walnut ink: Fiber Scraps
Other: Jute and scrim

HOW TO: Print birthday definition onto Ledger paper and trim and tear to size. Attach diagonally across the front center of card. Wrap a small rectangle of patterned paper around lower right corner of Ledger paper and secure with an eyelet. Set another eyelet in the upper left corner of definition block. Cut and tear same patterned paper to fit in lower left corner and a piece to slide behind and fold over definition. Crumple and flatten paper, fold in random places and secure with staples and adhesive. Tuck scrim under and over folded paper and definition and embellish with Charmed Word. Dye tag with walnut ink and let dry. Add Leather Flowers attached with mini brads to upper right corner of card and to tag. Wrap ribbon and jute through eyelets and around lower portion of card, stringing and knotting through hole in tag so that it is positioned along bottom edge. Lightly dust over card with brown stamping ink and a large stipple brush. TIME: 45 MINUTES

Friendship

CHAPTER

always there • the best shopper you know • wears the other half of your "best friends forever" charm necklace • needs a shoulder to cry on • crossed your mind today • wondering what she's up to • laughed at a funny joke and want to pass it on • can't remember the last time you talked • know she's stronger than she thinks she is • loves chocolate as much as you do

A few ways to make new friends and keep the old.

FOREVER FRIENDS
by mellette berezoski

Alphabet charms, blossoms, jelly label, mini brads, ribbon, scrapbook colors acrylic paint and tag with pocket card base and insert: Making Memories
Computer fonts: Miss Brooks downloaded from the Internet and Sans Serif by Microsoft Word

HOW TO: Print greeting on tag insert and stitch around edges with a sewing machine. Tie a ribbon through the hole at the top. Rub paint into two Alphabet Charms and wipe off excess. Cut a notch out of the card pocket on the left hand side. Mark on the tag where cut has been made and attach a large Blossom on the tag so that when it slides into the pocket, the flower lies directly over the notch. Attach another large Blossom to the right side of the pocket flap and place painted Alphabet Charms in the centers of both large flowers. Fill in the space between the two flowers with small Blossoms and attach with mini brads. Attach Jelly Label in the bottom right corner. TIME: 30 MINUTES

GIRLFRIEND
by kris stanger

Alphabet rub-ons, beads, blossoms, coastline embellishment paper, stitches and woven label: Making Memories

HOW TO: Trim paper to 9 x 8 inches and fold in half to create card. Starting 3 inches down from the top, cut a rectangle from the front flap measuring 2¾ x 1¼ inches. Using a sewing machine, zigzag stitch around the rectangle, fold card and apply alphabet rub-ons through the opening. Tie two lengths of Stitches around right side and knot. Create centers in two large Blossoms by stringing three small beads on a single stitch and knotting in the back. Attach Blossoms in the upper left corner. Attach Woven Label on top of a third Blossom. TIME: 15 MINUTES

Sisters Make The Best Girlfriends

thanks for being there for me

Friends Card

24

FRIENDSHIP
by lynne montgomery

CARD

Charmed word, jump rings, leather flowers, matchbook card base and insert, metal glue, mini brads, ribbon and scrapbook colors acrylic paint: Making Memories
Computer fonts: CK Simple by Creating Keepsakes and Tabitha
Rubber stamp: Hero Arts
Stamping ink: Ranger Industries
Other: Old book paper

ENVELOPE

Matchbook envelope, leather flower, metal glue, mini brads and scrapbook colors acrylic paint: Making Memories

HOW TO: Using acrylic paint, stamp script onto front of closed card, slightly overlapping top flap. Tear pieces from old book paper and attach to left side and top middle of card. Use flower mini brads to create centers in Leather Flowers. Using a paper piercer, make small holes on either side of bottom of card and in side petals of flowers. String three together using jump rings and embellish left side with two strips of ribbon. Tuck a small photo behind flower chain and add another Leather Flower to the top of the card. Create a stamp using a Leather Flower glued to a piece of wood large enough to grip. Apply paint to leather surface and stamp randomly over insert. When dry, print or write message. Clip the prongs off flower mini brads and glue flower parts to centers of stamped flowers. Close flap over insert, punch a hole through all layers and tie a ribbon through to secure. Rub paint into Charmed Word, wipe off excess and place over ribbon and book paper. Lightly dust front of card with brown stamping ink and stipple brush. TIME: 35 MINUTES

HOW TO: Using Leather Flower stamp and acrylic paint, stamp flower images randomly over front and back of envelope. Clip prongs off flower mini brads and glue flower parts to centers of stamped flowers. TIME: 10 MINUTES

without
rain

Encouragement Cards

WITHOUT RAIN
by julie turner

Blossoms, brad, ribbon words, scrapbook colors acrylic paint and stitches:
Making Memories
Computer font: Kabel by WordPerfect
Other: Transparency

HOW TO: Print the first half of message on bottom corner of
an 8½ x 11-inch transparency and cut in half to 8½ x 5½
inches. Fold in half to create outer card and crease the fold
with a bone folder. Edge transparency with paint, wrap a
length of Stitches around fold and knot. Set aside outer
card. Cut a 2¾ x 5½-inch rectangle out of a textured
cardstock and fold in half to make the small inside card.
Paint the outside and inside of mini card in complementary
colors and, when dry, lightly sand surface. With the fold of
the mini card on top, layer two Blossoms together and
attach to card with a brad. Cut a single word from Ribbon
Words and adhere to bottom of card, lining up edges.
Backstitch stem and leaves with Stitches to complete
flower. Print the second half of message on cardstock,
trim and place inside mini card. Position inner card inside
transparency and attach. TIME: 45 MINUTES

YOU
by lilac chang

Alphabet rub-ons, blossoms, buttons, charmed frame, defined, magnetic stamps
tin, moulding strips, ribbon, rub-ons, scrapbook colors acrylic paint, stamping ink
and tag: Making Memories
Key rings: Westrim Crafts
Other: Tulle and vellum

HOW TO: Paint the outside and inside of a Magnetic Stamps
tin in coordinating colors. Paint Moulding Strips in base
color and, when dry, dab paint to raised sections and paint
a Charmed Frame in same color as inside. Cut sections of
Defined stickers, ink edges and dab paint over surface. Stick
to vellum, tear around perimeters and edge with paint. Cut
a square of vellum and stitch around edges with sewing
machine. Layer vellum, Defined squares and painted frame
on front of tin and cut Moulding Strips to create a border
around all four edges. Apply alphabet rub-ons to a circle
vellum tag and dangle from two key rings looped together.
Tie small strips of ribbon to rings and knot a section of
tulle around one of the rings. Glue knot inside frame.
Create message inside with more rub-ons and Blossoms
embellished with button and ribbon centers.

TIME: 35 MINUTES

U
by jennifer jensen

Brads, eyelet charms, foam stamp, ledger paper, mini brads, rub-ons mini, safety pin, scrapbook colors acrylic paint, staples, stick pin, tag, upright window card base and woven label: Making Memories
Stamping ink: Ranger Industries
Other: Elastic, envelopes, rickrack and velveteen paper

HOW TO: Paint envelopes and heart Eyelet Charms in coordinating colors and set aside to dry. Cut a 1-inch slit on the inside fold of the card starting 2¾ inches down from the top. Thread a wide strip of ribbon through the slit around the inside to the outside and trim so that both ends slightly overhang edge of card. Glue a row of rickrack behind the top edge of the ribbon and attach the heart charms, tag and Woven Label with a variety of brads, elastic and pins. Secure end of wide ribbon on left side of card. Stamp letter on velveteen paper and place in window, adding a strip of rickrack along the top edge. Embellish small painted envelopes with ribbon, brads, rub-ons, staples and stamps, place inside the card where desired and secure. Tuck tags or folded Ledger paper inside with handwritten greetings and edge around entire card with brown ink. TIME: 40 MINUTES

THINKING OF YOU
by mellette berezoski

Computer font: Times New Roman by Microsoft Word
Double-dipped cardstock, ribbon charm and woven label: Making Memories
Other: Ribbon

HOW TO: Cut a 6-inch square of Double-Dipped cardstock. Fold in half and trim 1½ inches off the bottom of front flap. Print "you" six times onto cardstock using a combination of colors for the letters. Punch into squares, line up into two rows on the top flap and attach. Wrap ribbon around front flap, threading through a ribbon charm. Add Woven Label to bottom right corner. TIME: 25 MINUTES

Miss You Cards

FOREVER FRIENDS
by erin terrell

Charmed plaques mini, gatefold card base and
insert, jelly label, scrapbook colors acrylic paint
and woven corners: Making Memories
Other: Embossed paper

HOW TO: Trim floral embossed paper to
fit on card insert and use a foam brush
to rub paint over textured surface.
When dry, adhere to insert. Cut a
4-inch square of cardstock, edge with
paint, center over textured paper and
attach. Rub paint into plaques, wipe
off excess and mat with cardstock that
matches insert. Line along top of
center block and attach. Add Jelly
Label under plaques. Cut a strip
from card base, wrap around bottom
half and use string to secure. Add
Woven Labels in corners.

TIME: 15 MINUTES

I MISS YOU
by loni stevens

Definition: Pebbles Inc.
Paper: Li'l Davis Designs
Photo anchor, rub-ons mini, staple, upright slot card base and woven label: Making Memories
Square bubble letter and frame: Li'l Davis Designs
Other: Button, cardstock, embossed paper, flower and ribbon

HOW TO: Using a sewing machine, straight stitch along edges of slits on an upright
slot card. Fold in half to create a card and lightly sponge ink around edges. Cut
embossed paper to 3¼ x 4 inches, stitch around edges, slide through slot and
attach. Wrap ribbon around card, overlapping the slot and secure with a staple.
If desired, staple backwards so that prongs wrap around edges of ribbon. Add
flower on right side. Attach Woven Label, bubble letter and frame to bottom
and embellish with a Photo Anchor and button. Inside, cover top flap with map
patterned paper and bottom with cardstock, leaving a slight edge on all sides.
Add definition and rub-ons along bottom to complete. TIME: 40 MINUTES

Wedding

Inviting Love

CHAPTER 3

Tying The Knot

Showering the bride

Wishing a lifetime of Love and Happiness

Love and Wishes To Your Special Ones To Your Special

tying the knot · walking down the aisle · going to the chapel · sending love and wishes to the happy couple · showering the bride

· inviting loved ones to your special day · saving a date · saving a place · giving a gift · wishing a lifetime of love and happiness

· sharing wedded bliss · thanking for generosity and support · passing along wisdom and advice · starting a new life together

Cards and invitations that are as memorable as your wedding day.

YOU'RE INVITED
by lynne montgomery

CARD
Blossoms, eyelet letter, ribbon and tag with pocket
card base and insert: Making Memories
Buttons: Jesse James & Co.
Computer font: CBX Heber by Chatterbox
Fresco chalk ink pad: StampaRosa
Spray paint: Rust-Oleum
Other: Braided trim

HOW TO: Print "you're invited" onto
pocket and adhere braided trim along
bottom of folded section, wrapping
around to the back. Attach three
Blossoms to left side of pocket and
add buttons as centers. Print invitation
onto tag insert and softly ink around
edges with a chalk ink pad. Spray paint
an Eyelet Letter and, when dry, string
it onto ribbon. Tie ribbon in luggage-
tag style through hole in tag. Slide tag
insert into pocket base.

TIME: 20 MINUTES

ENVELOPE
Blossom, ribbon, patterned cardstock and tag with
pocket envelope: Making Memories
Button: Jesse James & Co.
Computer font: CBX Heber by Chatterbox

HOW TO: Print the names from the
guest list onto patterned cardstock that
matches the inside of the pocket and
cut into tag shapes. Punch a hole at the
top and loop ribbon through. Attach
Blossom over ribbon and add a button
as the center. Adhere embellished tag
to the front of the envelope.

TIME: 10 MINUTES

Wedding Invitations

MADELINE AND KEVIN
by julie turner

CARD

Decorative brad, scrapbook colors acrylic paint and scrapbook dye: Making Memories
Computer font: CK Elegant by Creating Keepsakes and Palatino by WordPerfect
Other: Embossed paper, silk organdy fabric and silk ribbon

HOW TO: Print invitation wording onto cardstock and trim to 5¾ x 4¼ inches. Print the initials of the bride and groom onto silk organdy fabric that measures 5¾ x 4¼ inches (hint: print the initials onto paper first, position and tape the fabric over the paper and run it through the printer again). Lay invitation at an angle on the embossed paper, fold in the sides and fold up the bottom and top. Experiment with scrap paper to create a template if desired. After folding, unfold and dip embossed paper into dye, blot dry and allow to dry overnight. Wet silk ribbon with water, lay flat on a paper towel and, using a foam brush, apply dye along one edge. Blot and iron to dry. Rub a coordinating color of paint into a Decorative Brad and wipe off excess. Layer invitation and organdy overlay on embossed paper, fold and tie ribbon around to hold closed. Wrap the prongs of the brad around the knot in the ribbon to finish. TIME: 25 MINUTES

ENVELOPE

Computer font: CK Elegant by Creating Keepsakes and Palatino by WordPerfect
Scrapbook dye: Making Memories
Other: Envelope

HOW TO: Dip the envelope flap into dye, blot and let dry. Print return address on the flap and the guest's address on the front. TIME: 5 MINUTES

FLOWER INVITATION
by mellette berezoski

Blossoms and decorative brad: Making Memories
Computer font: Edwardian Script downloaded from the Internet
Vellum: Chatterbox

HOW TO: Cut cardstock to 12 x 6 inches, fold into thirds and cut or punch a 2-inch window from the front flap of card. Print invitation information onto vellum and trim to fit middle section of card when fully opened. Trim a second piece of matching vellum to the same size. Layer three Blossoms and attach to vellum with a Decorative Brad so that flowers are visible through front opening. Adhere printed piece to inside and embellished piece to second flap of card. Wrap and tie ribbon around card to hold closed.

TIME: 15 MINUTES

YOU'RE INVITED
by lilac chang

Blossoms, cardstock, decorative brads, jelly label, label holder, magnetic date stamp, mini brads, scrapbook colors acrylic paint, stitched tin tile and vellum: Making Memories
Paper: 7Gypsies
Woven paper: Creative Imaginations

HOW TO: Cut a 2½-inch strip of patterned paper. Trim edges to fit the width of the card. Brush paint over paper and a Stitched Tin Tile. Rub paint into four Decorative Brads, wipe away excess and set all painted pieces aside to dry. Trim cardstock to 7¾ x 9¼ inches and fold in half so that pattern is on the outside. Trim a piece of vellum to fit over the front flap and tear away right side. Stitch it to flap using a sewing machine. Cut a 3½-inch strip of woven paper and fray edges. Place on card and layer painted paper on top. Stitch across top and bottom edges to secure and place Decorative Brads in each corner. Whipstitch around painted tile and center on paper over two Blossoms. Adhere all pieces and add a Jelly Label to the top. Attach label holder to bottom right corner and stamp date inside. TIME: 20 MINUTES

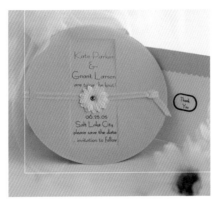

CELEBRATE LOVE
by jennifer jensen

INVITATION

Blossom, mini brads, rub-ons mini and tag:
Making Memories
Computer font: Bernhard Fashion BT by WordPerfect
Paper: Lasting Impressions
Other: Grosgrain ribbon, jeweled fastener and tulle

HOW TO: Fold in 1¾ inches from the
left edge of an 8½ x 11-inch sheet
of paper. Tack down a 16-inch piece
of ribbon across the patterned side of
paper starting 2 inches down from
the top and stitch around the entire
perimeter to create an inside pocket.
Fold in half to create card. Layer
Blossoms and tulle onto a circle tag
and attach through center with a
jeweled fastener. Adhere to ribbon
and apply rub-on just below. Print
wedding information onto cardstock
and trim to 4½ x 6¼ inches. Mat with
colored cardstock, attach together with
brads and slide into left inside pocket.
Print RSVP card and trim to fit inside
small envelope. Print return address
on envelope, embellish with magnetic
stamp and slide both pieces into right
inside pocket. TIME: 15 MINUTES

SAVE THE DATE

Blossoms, mini brad and ribbon: Making Memories
Computer font: Bernhard Fashion BT by WordPerfect
Other: Patterned vellum

HOW TO: Print information onto
cardstock and cut into a 5½-inch
circle. Cut a piece of patterned vellum
to the same size and cut out a window
so that printed information is visible
through opening. Cut two slits on
either side of circle and thread and
tie ribbon through. Layer two small
Blossoms together and attach over
ribbon with a brad. TIME: 15 MINUTES

THANK YOU CARD

Artisan label: Making Memories
Computer font: Bernhard Fashion BT by WordPerfect
Decorative scissors: Fiskars

HOW TO: Cut a piece of cardstock to
4⅞ x 6⅞ inches and fold in half. Cut
a 1-inch strip of colored cardstock,
trim edge with decorative scissors,
adhere along fold and trim to fit
width of card. Print message onto
Artisan Label and apply to front flap.
TIME: 5 MINUTES

PLACE CARD (template included)

Magnetic stamps and mini brad: Making Memories
Computer font: Bernhard Fashion BT by WordPerfect
Decorative scissors: Fiskars

HOW TO: Print guest's name onto
cardstock, stamp decorative images
underneath and trim to 3½ x 4 inches
so that text appears in the bottom half
of the rectangle. Cut colored cardstock
to 3½ x 5¾ inches. Trim one of the
short ends with decorative scissors,
place both pieces together lining up
bottom edges and fold long edge of
colored cardstock over to front. Adhere
and secure with a brad through both
layers. Round bottom corners of
both flaps. TIME: 5 MINUTES

celebrate
love

Wedding Events

CELEBRATE LOVE
by kris stanger

Blossoms, foam stamp, latch card base and insert, mini brads, ribbon, ribbon charm, scrapbook colors acrylic paint and woven label: Making Memories Other: Hat pin

HOW TO: Trim 1¼ inches off one edge of the insert. Dry brush paint onto edges and front of card and insert. Stamp decorative images along right edge inside the card base with paint. Cut a 2 x 1-inch opening into insert starting ⅝ inch down from the top. Cut a small piece of cardstock in a complementary color, adhere it behind the window and center a Woven Label so that both pieces are visible. Wrap a piece of ribbon around left side of opening securing on the back and attach a Blossom to the side using a brad. Adhere insert inside card so that right edge lines up with right edge of the front flap. Cut a 2¾ x 1¾-inch opening in the front flap of the card starting ½ inch from the top. Embellishments on the insert should be visible through the opening. Paint the edges of a ribbon charm and wipe away excess. Tie a ribbon around the left edge of the front flap and tie through the charm. Layer two Blossoms together using a brad to secure and attach just above the latch slot with a hat pin. Dab paint on both brads to finish.

TIME: 25 MINUTES

FOREVER LOVE
by erin terrell

Cardstock tag, charmed plaques mini, double-dipped cardstock, eyelet, jump ring, ribbon, rub-ons and upright window card base and insert: Making Memories Spray paint: Krylon

HOW TO: Sand the plaques and apply an even coat of spray paint. Set aside to dry. Cut several strips of cardstock in coordinating colors, attach to bottom of card and trim to fit. Apply rub-ons to strips. Wrap three strands of ribbon around the right side of card and through the window opening, knotting on the front. Set an eyelet through the hole in the Cardstock Tag, loop a jump ring through and dangle from the bottom ribbon. Adhere insert to inside of card, close and attach one painted plaque to the insert so that it is centered in the opening. Attach second plaque to bottom of card, overlapping paper strips.

TIME: 10 MINUTES

Love

CHAPTER 4

Still Makes You Laugh

No Reason Whatsoever

You Haven't Told Him Lately

you haven't told him lately · gave you a day all to yourself · sometimes it's easier to write it than to say it · no reason whatsoever · just thought he'd like to know · sent you flowers · sending him flowers · shared years of memories · stuck together · through better and worse · still makes you laugh · as handsome today as the day you got married

Don't just say those three little words–shout them.

LOVE WHO?
by kris stanger

Alphabet rub-ons, cardstock tags, charmed plaque mini, decorative brads, jelly label, magnetic stamp, mini brads, ribbon, rub-ons, scrapbook colors acrylic paint, shaped clip and tag with pocket card base and insert: Making Memories Stamping ink: Stampin' Up!

HOW TO: Cut out a heart large enough to cover the front flap of the card. Cut off the left third and ink around both pieces with brown stamping ink. Edge base and insert with ink. Punch small holes along cut edges of heart and tie together with ribbon. Apply alphabet rub-ons to front and attach a small, inked tag with a brad. Adhere heart to card and attach a Shaped Clip to the flap so that it sits behind the right side of the heart. Cut a strip of ribbon, place over the hole on the tag insert and secure with a Decorative Brad. Attach Jelly Label and apply rub-ons to complete inside greeting. Cut a ½-inch strip of cardstock that matches the heart, place on the bottom of the tag and secure with four brads. Edge a Charmed Plaque Mini with paint and attach to the center of the strip. TIME: 25 MINUTES

LOVE BLOCKS
by mellette berezoski

CARD
Foam stamps, ledger paper, mini brad, moulding corner, photo anchor, ribbon, scrapbook colors acrylic paint, staples and woven label: Making Memories

HOW TO: Cut two pieces of cardstock to fit inside envelope. Punch six holes along top edge and tie pieces together with a variety of coordinating ribbon. Punch or cut four squares of the same size from Ledger paper to fit front of card. Using foam stamps and paint, stamp three squares with letters. For the "O", substitute a circle Woven Label. Embellish the blocks with staples, a Moulding Corner and a Photo Anchor secured with a brad. Cut a piece of Ledger paper to fit the inside for a written greeting.
TIME: 30 MINUTES

ENVELOPE
Envelope template: Deluxe Designs
Ledger paper, ribbon, rub-on, staples and washer words: Making Memories

HOW TO: Use template to trace and cut out envelope from cardstock. Trim Ledger paper to fit the top flap and staple in top corners. Punch two holes in the top and bottom flaps, attach Washer Words lining up holes and tie ribbon through. Apply rub-on to bottom right corner.
TIME: 15 MINUTES

Love Card

KISS
by lynne montgomery

CARD

Alphabet charm, decorative brad, eyelet letter, jump rings, ribbon, scrapbook colors
acrylic paint, stamping ink and upright window envelope: Making Memories
Bingo letter: Li'l Davis Designs
Clip art: Art Chix Studio
Computer font: Times New Roman by Microsoft Word
Decoupage and collage gel: Hot Off the Press
Metal button: Rusty Pickle
Paper: Anna Griffin
Tag punch: Punch Woodward
Other: Braided trim, charm, old book paper and shipping tags

HOW TO: Adhere patterned paper to the front of an upright window envelope and a coordinating patterned paper to the flaps on the back. Fold envelope in half so that the front of the envelope is the outside. The end with the large flap is the top of the card. Lightly ink around all edges. Tear a heart shape from old book paper and center just above fold. Dry brush cream paint over surface of card and decoupage clipped words to heart. Paint an Eyelet Letter and edge with ink. Rub paint into an Alphabet Charm and wipe away excess. Attach letters and charm just above the heart to create title and tie ribbon to charm. Set metal button to the center of the large flap. Open card and with a craft knife, separate seam of envelope on the left side big enough to fit several shipping tags. Attach braided trim along seam to cover. Mat a vintage photo with layers of crumpled and inked book paper and patterned paper. Adhere to right side of card. Attach book paper to cardstock and punch three tag shapes. Ink edges, decoupage text onto tags and dangle from trim with jump rings. Create a mini book with several shipping tags. Cover the front tag with patterned paper, ink edges and decoupage text on front. Secure book with a Decorative Brad through the holes and slip into separated seam. TIME: 45 MINUTES

ENVELOPE

Jump ring, matchook envelope and ribbon:
Making Memories
Other: Charm

HOW TO: Place several layers of paper or a mat slightly inside envelope and cut three sets of slits ½ inch below fold. Wrap ribbon around back, weave through slits in front and tie a bow on the right side. Dangle a heart charm from a jump ring through the bow.
TIME: 15 MINUTES

BE MINE FOREVER

by erin terrell

Blossom, decorative brads, double-dipped cardstock, matchbook card base and insert, ribbon, snaps, woven corners and woven labels: Making Memories
Circle punch: McGill
Stamping ink: Memories

HOW TO: Trim a piece of cardstock to fit onto insert, leaving a border around all edges. Ink the edges of insert. Add Woven Corners and Woven Labels to cardstock, slightly overlapping the largest label onto insert. Set three snaps along both edges of large label and attach Blossom with a Decorative Brad just below label on the left side. Attach embellished insert to inside of base. For the outside, trim cardstock to fit the large flap leaving a ½-inch border around edges. Punch a circle from the center of piece, just above bottom edge. Lightly ink edges of both pieces and attach. Place Decorative Brads in the middle of circles and tie ribbon around one side. Use ribbon to wrap around brads to close. TIME: 15 MINUTES

2 EVERLASTING LOVE

by lilac chang

Blossom, cardstock tag, defined, jelly label, latch card base, mini brads, photo anchors, ribbon, safety pin, scrapbook colors acrylic paint and staples: Making Memories
Charm: Embellish It!
Paper: 7 Gypsies
Stamping ink: Ranger Industries
Other: Bingo number, burlap, denim and vellum envelope

HOW TO: Adhere burlap to front flap of card with spray adhesive. Paint patterned paper and before dry, wipe off excess so pattern is visible. Tear a strip and staple along left edge. Paint the inside of a vellum envelope, let dry and attach to center of flap. Embellish with a lightly painted Blossom and bingo number and ink edges of Defined strips to slide inside. Cut a small piece of denim and adhere to latch. Punch hole in left side of denim, tie ribbon through and dangle a charm from ribbon with a safety pin. Attach Jelly Label at an angle to denim latch. Place three Photo Anchors along right side of flap and secure with mini brads, dangling Cardstock Tag from the top one. TIME: 20 MINUTES

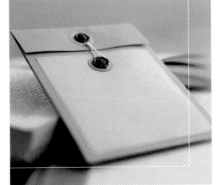

Baby

CHAPTER 5

announcing an arrival · showering love · nine long months of anticipation · welcoming to the world · who wouldn't want to see your new baby? · created a life · created a family · couldn't be happier · preparing the nursery · preparing the parents · spreading the news · spreading the joy · he's finally here · she's gorgeous

Give a brand new life a grand entrance.

BABY SHOWER
by lynne montgomery

CARD (template included)
Alphabet stamps: StampaRosa
Charmed plaque mini, classic small card base,
double-dipped cardstock, label holder, ribbon,
safety pin, scrapbook colors acrylic paint, snaps and
staples: Making Memories
Stamping ink: Ranger Industries
Other: Old book paper, shipping tag and twill tape

HOW TO: Trace the tabs from a manila
file folder onto card base, cut out and
ink all edges. Stitch around the sides
and fold of the card and stamp message
onto tab. Zigzag stitch down a length
of twill tape. Rub paint into grooves
of Charmed Plaque Mini, wipe away
excess and paint a label holder. Layer
painted pieces onto twill tape and
attach with snaps. Wrap twill tape
around card and tie closed. Adhere
if desired. Glue old book paper to a
shipping tag and dry brush with acrylic
paint. Print shower information onto
cardstock, cut into strips and attach to
tag with staples. Attach ribbon through
hole with a safety pin. TIME: 30 MINUTES

ENVELOPE (template included)
Classic small envelope, double-dipped cardstock,
safety pin and staples: Making Memories
Other: Old book paper, shipping tag and twill tape

HOW TO: Zigzag stitch down a length
of twill tape, wrap around envelope
and adhere. Glue old book paper to a
small shipping tag, dry brush and tear
off bottom. Print guest's name onto
cardstock and attach to tag with staples.
Attach tag to twill tape with a safety
pin. TIME: 15 MINUTES

54

56

sweet baby

Baby Announcements

EMMA MARIE
by julie turner

CD label: Avery
Computer font: BernhardMod by WordPerfect
Gatefold card base, scrapbook colors acrylic paint and snaps: Making Memories
Ribbon: Bucilla
Other: Fabric and silk flowers

HOW TO: Lightly wipe the folded edges of the card with paint. Create the band that wraps around the card by cutting a 2 x 12-inch strip of cardstock. Fold the cardstock lengthwise to make decorative creases in the paper. Wrap the band around the card and mark and cut slits where the ends overlap to make a closure. Tie a strip of ribbon to the left side of the band. Embellish the right side by layering strips of ribbon, a scrap of tulle and silk flowers. Clip off the back of a heart snap and glue the heart to the bottom left corner. For the inside, cut a piece of fabric to fit and adhere with spray adhesive. Print information on the fabric and add a heart, flower and ribbon to the inside flaps. Create a CD label and adhere to a CD that contains photos or video. Lay ribbon diagonally across the middle section of the card and secure each end with a snap. Slide CD behind the ribbon, close card and wrap band around card to hold together.

TIME: 30 MINUTES

SWEET BABY
by mellette berezoski

Brads, charmed plaque mini, foam stamp, rub-ons mini, scrapbook colors acrylic paint and staple: Making Memories
Computer fonts: Avant Garde and Mariette downloaded from the Internet
Paper: Chatterbox
Other: Lace

HOW TO: Create pocket by cutting a piece of cardstock to $4\frac{1}{4}$ x $5\frac{1}{4}$ inches. Cut a piece of double-sided paper to $4\frac{3}{4}$ x 5 inches. Cut one edge of the shorter length with decorative scissors and fold down so that both sides of paper show. Place on the piece of cardstock so that edges slightly overhang on three sides. Fold edges around to the back of the cardstock, adhere and add brads on either side of folded border to form the pocket. Stamp initial with acrylic paint in bottom right corner and, when dry, apply rub-on over the top. Rub paint into a Charmed Plaque Mini, wipe away excess and set aside to dry. Cut a piece of cardstock to $3\frac{1}{2}$ x $5\frac{1}{2}$ inches. Print announcement information onto decorative vellum and trim to $3\frac{1}{2}$ x $5\frac{1}{2}$ inches. Place over cardstock, staple a strip of lace to the top middle and attach painted plaque above text. Trim top corners to create a tag shape and slide into pocket.

TIME: 30 MINUTES

57

Announcing the arrival of our daughter, Jordan
Rae Brooksby, born April 29, 2002 at Mesa
General Hospital in Mesa, Arizona. Weighing
7lbs. and measuring 19 inches long.

Proud Parents:
Nolan & Mindy Brooksby

iNtR
Oduc
iNg...

Our sweet baby girl.

baby girl

ANNOUNCING

Baby Announcements

ANNOUNCING BABY GIRL
by robin johnson

Cardstock tags, ribbon and safety pins:
Making Memories
Computer fonts: Garamond, English III and
Presto BT

HOW TO: Print title on the cover
positioning text in lower half of card
to allow for photo above. Print the
inside text using the same fonts, again
in the lower half of the card. Position
baby's name so that it will appear right
under inside photo. Once printed,
trim cardstock to 10 x 5 inches and
fold to create a card. Print photos in
wallet size, trim, mat and attach. Tie
ribbon around fold, stringing on a
Cardstock Tag before knotting.
Embellish with a safety pin. On the
inside, tie a small knot in the center
of another tag, add safety pin and
attach on the right side of the photo.

TIME: 15 MINUTES

INTRODUCING
by loni stevens

Alphabet rub-ons, eyelets, jump rings and upright
slot card and insert: Making Memories
Computer font: Avant Garde by Microsoft Word
Laminate film: Duck by Henkel
Multi-surface chalk ink: VersaMagic by Tsukineko
Other: Charm, metal ruler, ribbon and trim

HOW TO: Cut a piece of vellum to the
width of an upright slot card and trim
to 6½ inches long. Apply rub-ons to
center of bottom half and stitch a
square around text with a sewing
machine. Print text strip in reverse,
trim and adhere along bottom stitch.
Run the vellum piece through a home
or commercial laminating machine.
Poke holes on either side of text strip,
loop jump rings through and dangle a
charm from the left side. Line card
and laminated piece up along top
edge, punch two holes, set eyelets and
attach pieces together with jump rings.
Attach ribbon and trim to slot and
print information on top of insert.
Arrange photos and metal ruler piece
on the bottom of insert and adhere.
Slide insert through slot and adhere.

TIME: 35 MINUTES

JUNE 2003
by kris stanger

Charmed frame, jump rings, mini brad, mini tag,
moulding strip, ribbon, rub-ons mini, safety pin and
scrapbook colors acrylic paint: Making Memories
Ribbon: Bucilla
Other: Heart charm

HOW TO: Paint frame and Moulding
Strip with base color and gently rub a
lighter color over the top. Set aside to
dry. Cut cardstock to 11 x 5¼ inches
and create a tri-fold card so that the
front flap measures 3 inches. Attach
painted strip along edge of front flap.
Place photo behind painted frame, tie
ribbon around edge, including a safety
pin in the knot. From the safety pin,
dangle a charm from two jump rings.
Attach embellished frame to top center
of left side on the front flap. Rub
paint into a mini tag, wipe away
excess and attach just below frame
with a brad. Dab paint onto brad with
coordinating color. Apply rub-on to
bottom right corner and tie ribbon
around card to hold together. Add
more photos and information inside.

TIME: 20 MINUTES

WELCOME HOME
by jennifer jensen

Cardstock tags, classic small card base and insert, magnetic stamps, staple and tags: Making Memories
Decorative scissors: Fiskars
Other: Buttons, patterned paper, ribbon, tulle and vellum envelope

HOW TO: Trim a thin strip from the front flap of a card base and sew around three sides with a sewing machine. With a craft knife, make a slit in the bottom of the vellum envelope and slide a piece of patterned paper through so that the ends stick out on either end. Adhere to the center front of the card. Cut or punch three flower shapes from patterned paper and solid papers and attach to an oval tag. Slightly fold up petals to create dimension. Layer tulle and buttons for the center. Punch a hole in the tag opposite the existing hole and thread and knot ribbon through both sides. Attach embellished tag to vellum envelope and tuck several Cardstock Tags under metal rim. Secure with a small amount of glue. Trim the right edge of the insert with decorative scissors and place inside so that the edge is visible when the card is closed. Stitch around insert with a sewing machine. Stamp ornamental images along the top of the insert. Embellish a small tag with matching ribbon, paper and a Cardstock Tag, securing layers to card with a staple. TIME: 20 MINUTES

Expressions

CHAPTER
6

listened to you · encouraged you · paid for your lunch · had you for dinner · gave you cashmere · couldn't have done it without her · never been more proud · a major accomplishment · aced a test · heard the news · new job promotion · baby on the way · why not? · brighten a day · strengthen a friendship

Express yourself with your message and your design.

64

Congratulations Card

CONGRATS
by kris stanger

CARD
Alphabet charm, alphabet rub-ons, brads, button, classic small card base and insert, eyelet charm, jigsaw alphabet, mailbox alphabet, scrapbook colors acrylic paint and tag: Making Memories
Paper: Bazzill
Rickrack: Wright's
Other: Ribbon

HOW TO: Punch out Jigsaw Alphabet letters and paint. Rub paint into an Alphabet Charm, wipe away excess and paint a square Eyelet Charm. Let all pieces dry. Cut a strip of paper to 5½ x 2⅛ inches. Create greeting on the strip using a Mailbox Alphabet letter, a tag and brad, ribbon strips, painted Jigsaw Alphabet letters, alphabet rub-ons on painted Eyelet Charm and a layered button and Alphabet Charm. Adhere embellished strip to front of card, ¾ inch down from the fold. Cut two more strips from paper measuring 5½ x ½ and 5½ x ¼ inches and attach below embellished strip. Wrap rickrack around the bottom edge of middle strip and secure on the back. Attach insert inside. TIME: 20 MINUTES

ENVELOPE
Classic small envelope, mini brad and photo anchor: Making Memories
Paper: Bazzill
Other: Ribbon

HOW TO: Cut a strip of paper that measures 6½ x 2⅛ inches. Fold back 1 inch on either end of strip and punch two holes on both flaps. Wrap strip around the flap end of the envelope and attach. Lace ribbon through holes and knot. Poke a small hole in the center of the flap and add a Photo Anchor and brad to embellish.

TIME: 10 MINUTES

CONGRATULATIONS
by julie turner

CARD
Charmed word and jelly label: Making Memories
Clear sticker labels: Avery
Other: Cardstock and translucent plastic from a report cover

HOW TO: Cut a piece of translucent plastic to a 4¾-inch square. Print "success" onto cardstock and punch out using a 1½-inch circle punch. Using the same punch, punch eight more circles from several colors of cardstock, arrange all nine into three rows starting in bottom left corner and adhere to plastic background. Place Jelly Label along right edge and Charmed Word over bottom two circles. Print definition onto a clear label sticker using the mirror-image setting so that text is readable from the front of the card. Carefully apply sticker to back of plastic piece so that definition appears along top edge. TIME: 15 MINUTES

ENVELOPE (template included)
Eyelets: Making Memories
Other: Die cut 5x5 petal-style envelope and string

HOW TO: Punch two more circles from matching cardstock. Place on either side of envelope flaps and set eyelets in the middle. Tie string around one side and use to wrap around circles for the closure. TIME: 5 MINUTES

MERCI
by erin terrell

Blossoms, brads, double-dipped cardstock, foam stamps, jelly label, label holder, mini brads, ribbon, scrapbook colors acrylic paint and upright window card base: Making Memories

HOW TO: Cut a piece of cardstock to 3¼ x 2 inches and lightly sand surface. Adhere to front of card along right edge. Place Jelly Label along bottom edge of cardstock, lay label holder over the top and secure by looping ribbon through holes and wrapping around. Using acrylic paint, stamp a decorative image onto corner of cardstock, overlapping slightly onto card. To complete inside, cut two 3⅞-inch square pieces of cardstock and two strips in a complementary color. Attach strips to squares along bottom edges and lightly sand both pieces. Using brads, attach three Blossoms in the bottom left corner of one block and adhere both blocks to the inside of the card. Trim any that overhangs edges. Cut another piece of cardstock to 3¼ x 1¾ inches. Lightly sand and adhere 1⅛ inches above block on the right inside flap. Stamp greeting and decorative image onto cardstock pieces using acrylic paint. Attach Blossom with a brad so that it is slightly visible through the window when the card is closed. TIME: 15 MINUTES

THANK YOU
by lilac chang

Blossoms, mini brad, jelly label, ribbon and upright slot card base and insert: Making Memories

HOW TO: Wrap and knot three coordinating strands of ribbon around the top section of an upright slot card. Turn over and slide insert through slots so that it covers the back of the ribbon and attach at all corners. Layer two Blossoms in the bottom right corner of the insert and secure with a brad through the center. At the bottom slit of the slot, fold card over so that knotted ribbon side is now the front flap of the card. Add a Jelly Label just below ribbon to finish.

TIME: 10 MINUTES

Thank You Cards

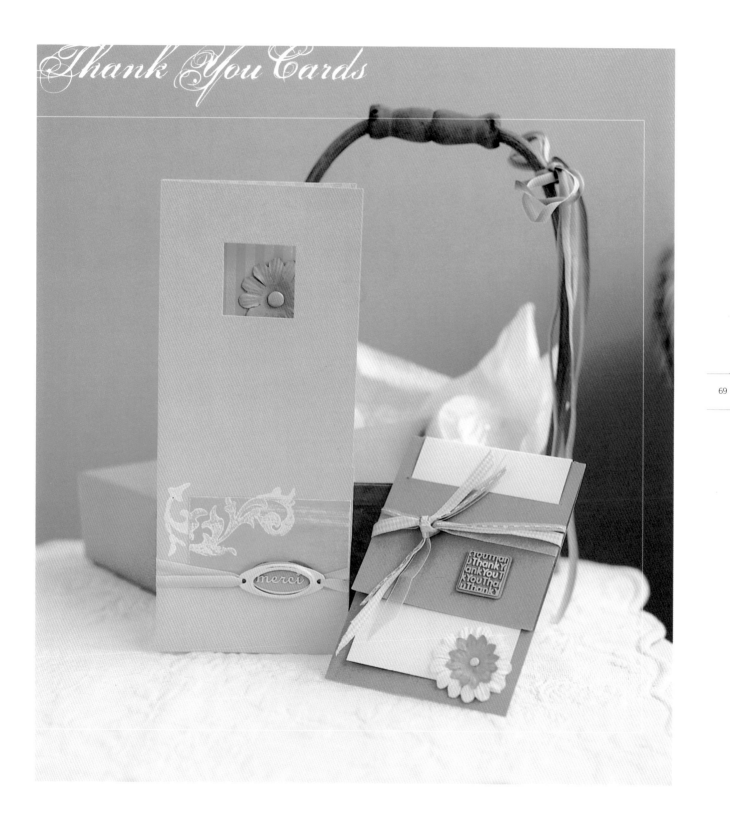

DANKE, GRACIAS, GRAZIE, ARIGATO, THANKS, MERCI
by mellette berezoski

CARD

Canvas paper: Canson
Computer fonts: Evergreen, Fancy Free, Fat Frog, Tasklist and Typo downloaded from twopeasinabucket.com
Matchbook card base and insert, mini brad, ribbon, scrapbook colors acrylic paint and woven label:
Making Memories

HOW TO: Paint canvas paper with five different colors of acrylic paint. Print text onto paper so that each word appears on a different color and cut into ½-inch strips. Sew a 4-inch background square onto front flap of card and arrange strips on top so that words are staggered. Attach strips, trim to fit card and tie matching ribbon around three of the strips. Print inside greeting onto cardstock, trim and sew to insert. Poke a hole in the bottom of the Woven Label and attach through the bottom flap and insert with a brad. Tuck in front flap. TIME: 25 MINUTES

ENVELOPE

Matchbook envelope, rub-ons mini, scrapbook colors acrylic paint and woven label: Making Memories
Canvas paper: Canson

HOW TO: Trace envelope flaps onto cardstock, cut out, attach and draw lines around edges to mimic stitching. Paint canvas paper in two complementary colors and cut out two circles, one larger than the other. Adhere larger circle under flap and smaller circle and Woven Label on top of flap. Apply rub-on above flap in bottom right corner. TIME: 15 MINUTES

71

Sympathy

CHAPTER 7

Healing a Wound

Wanting To Help

Showing Support

too far away to hug · wanting to help · grieving with them · going through a tough time · need you like never before · feeling blue · feeling sick · feeling their pain · visiting the hospital · minor accident · major accident · fighting a disease · dealing with heartache · showing support · healing a wound · letting them know that, in time, this too shall pass

Show that you care even when times are tough.

HOPE

by jennifer jensen

Adhesive: Diamond Glaze
Artisan labels, brads, label holder, magnetic stamps, mini brad, photo flips, ribbon, scrapbook colors acrylic paint and upright slot card base and insert: Making Memories
Paper: Bazzill
Other: Ribbon and stamping ink

HOW TO: Cut card base ¼ inch from short side of the slot. Print inside message onto insert, trim to fit new size of card, slide through slot and adhere. Add Artisan Label and painted brad to top of message. Cut a piece of cardstock to 3⅜ x 5¼ inches and edge with ink. Place Artisan Label in the middle of piece and stamp with message and decorative stamps. Smear paint onto Photo Flips and, when dry, use to attach cardstock on top of the insert. Attach a label holder to the middle of the slot, securing with ribbon. Dab paint onto three heart-shaped brads, cut off prongs and glue in the opening. Fill in area with Diamond Glaze and let dry. TIME: 20 MINUTES

SO SORRY FOR YOUR LOSS

by erin terrell

Blossoms, brad, matchbook card base and insert, mini brad and ribbon: Making Memories
Computer font: AL Highlight downloaded from twopeasinabucket.com
Stamping ink: Colorbox
Other: Shipping tag and walnut ink

HOW TO: Dip small shipping tag in walnut ink and set aside to dry. Print message on insert and card. Trim insert to 3¼ x 4½ inches. Edge insert with ink, wrap the dyed tag around the top and tie through with a ribbon. Attach Blossoms to top right corner of insert with brads and tie card together with two lengths of coordinating ribbon.

TIME: 15 MINUTES

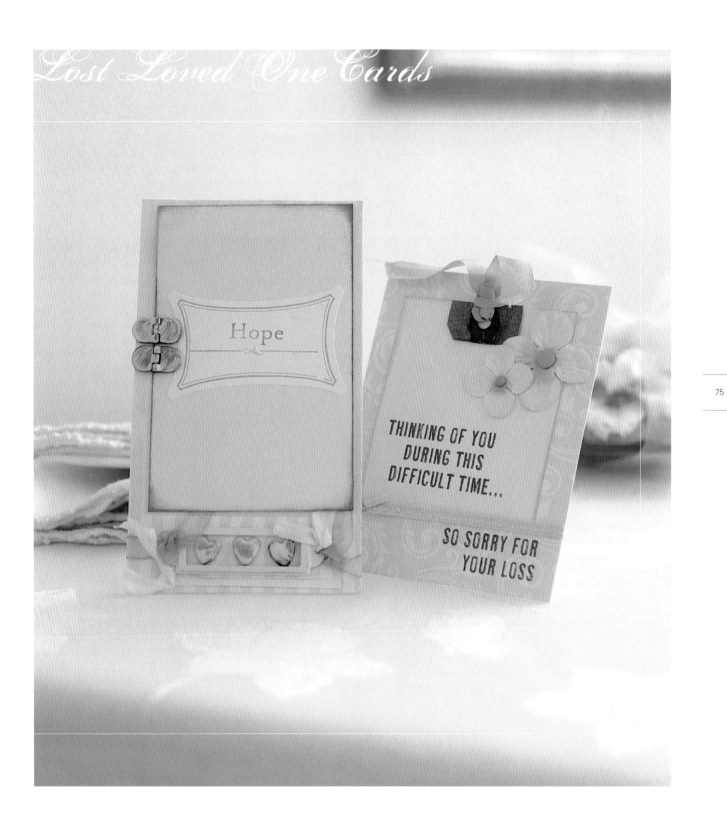

THINKING OF YOU
by kris stanger

CARD
Alphabet stamps: PSX Design
Computer font: Bernhardt Fashion by Microsoft Word
Eyelet letter, jelly label, label holder, magnetic stamp, mini brads, scrapbook colors acrylic paint, upright slot card base and insert and woven corners: Making Memories
Ribbon: Bucilla
Other: Heart stamp, muslin and twill tape

HOW TO: Print message onto muslin and fray to fit on insert. Slide through slot, and adhere to card using Woven Corners. Paint Eyelet Letter, let dry and use as first letter in recipient's name. Complete names using alphabet stamps, heart stamp and paint. Stamp three decorative images onto twill tape and attach diagonally across card using brads. Place Jelly Label in the middle of the slot, lay label holder on top and secure by tying and knotting ribbon through holes and around edges of card. TIME: 15 MINUTES

ENVELOPE
Alphabet rub-ons, magnetic stamp, mini brads, scrapbook colors acrylic paint, upright slot envelope: Making Memories
Other: Twill tape

HOW TO: Edge envelope with paint and brush several strokes down the seam. Stamp decorative images down the center of the back and along a small strip of twill tape. Punch a small hole in the center of the flap, thread twill tape through and knot. Glue the end under the flap to secure. Dab paint onto the heads of two brads and place beneath the knot. Apply rub-ons across the bottom of the envelope and decorate with small dots of paint.
TIME: 5 MINUTES

GET WELL
by lilac chang

Blossom, cardstock tag, cosmopolitan embellishment paper, foam stamp, jump rings, ribbon, scrapbook colors acrylic paint, snap and tags: Making Memories

HOW TO: Cut paper to 12 x 6 inches, lightly sand surface and fold to create a tri-fold card. Measure and cut a circle in the middle of both flaps the size of the round tags. Remove the centers of tags and attach metal rims around circles. Attach a Blossom on the inside of the card with a snap so that flower is visible through the opening. Wrap three strands of ribbon around top and through tag opening on front flap, knotting to secure. Brush paint across a square vellum tag and stamp with foam stamp and paint. Fold around the bottom edge of card and adhere. String three jump rings together and use to dangle a Cardstock Tag from the ribbon. Write greeting on tag. TIME: 15 MINUTES

  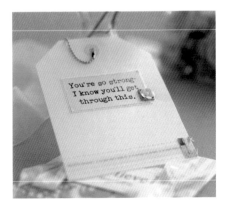

HOPE
by mellette berezoski

Charmed photo corners, charmed word and classic
small card base and insert: Making Memories
Computer fonts: 1942 Report, Avant Garde, Carpenter
and Courier all downloaded from the Internet
Photo sticker: Pebbles Inc.
Vellum: Stampin' Up!
Other: Jute

HOW TO: Apply sticker to the middle
of the front flap of card. Print words
and phrases onto vellum in grayscale
for the background and black for the
title. Trim to the same size as the card,
fold around to create an overlay and
punch two holes in the folds. Tie jute
through to join together and add
Charmed Word to bottom right corner
of vellum. Print message onto insert,
adhere to inside and add photo corners
to top left and bottom right corners.

TIME: 25 MINUTES

BELIEVE
by loni stevens

Bead chain, defined, eyelet, staple and tag with pocket card base and insert: Making Memories
Computer font: Acoustic Light downloaded from the Internet
Concho: Scrapworks
Fabric: Junkitz
Flower: Savvy Stamps
Other: Ribbon

HOW TO: Cut a piece of fabric to fit the bottom half of the card base. Stitch
around the edges to secure. Adhere a strip of ribbon around the pocket where
the fabric and paper meet to cover the seam. Apply Defined sticker to cardstock
and trim to leave a slight border. Stitch around perimeter and adhere piece to
the middle of the pocket. Tie two bows with the ribbon and adhere to either side
of the definition. Set an eyelet in the tag hole and loop a length of bead chain
through. Print message onto cardstock, tear edges and mat with another piece
of cardstock. Trim edges, leaving a border. Place a concho in the right bottom
corner and embellish with a small flower inside. Adhere to tag insert. Apply
Defined sticker strip across the bottom of the tag, stitch with a sewing machine
on either side and wrap a small scrap of fabric around right edge, securing
with a staple. TIME: 25 MINUTES

Holidays

CHAPTER

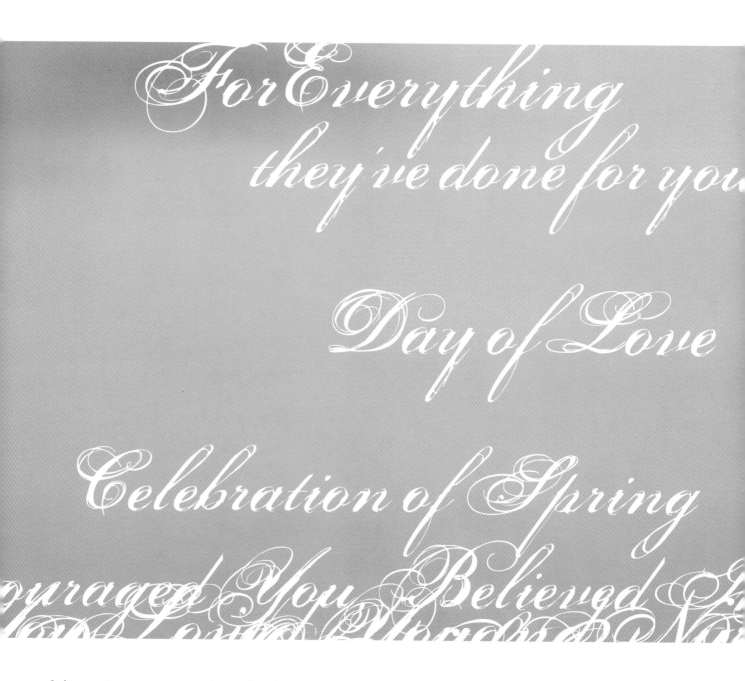

For Everything

they've done for you

Day of Love

Celebration of Spring

feeling passion · wanting a sweetheart · day of love · cupid's arrow · new beginnings · waiting for a visit from the bunny · giving a basket · celebration of spring · for everything they've done for you · she's your mom · he's your dad · she kissed it all better · he made you get up again · she hugged you, loved you and nurtured you · he encouraged you, believed in you and challenged you

Celebrate the holidays throughout the year with warmth and love.

KISS ME
by lilac chang

Alpha fetti, cardstock tag, jigsaw alphabet,
scrapbook colors acrylic paint and stamping ink:
Making Memories
Other: D-rings and ribbon

HOW TO: Trim a piece of cardstock to
6 x 10 inches and fold in half. Paint
four Jigsaw Alphabet letters in two
complementary colors and, when dry,
sand edges of blocks and letters until
pieces look worn. Lay two types of
ribbon across the middle of the card
and adhere. Adhere letters on top
of the ribbon in two rows. Edge
Cardstock Tag with ink and dangle
from a d-ring. Tie two d-rings to the
ends of the ribbon on the left side of
the card so that rings fall in the middle
of the letters. Trim ends short. Bring
ribbon on the right side through the
d-rings and cinch tight. Lightly sand
Alpha Fetti letters and place in the
bottom right corner. TIME: 20 MINUTES

LOVE
by jennifer jensen

Artisan label, classic small card base, decorative brads, defined clear, eyelet charm, foam stamp, hinge,
mini brads, ribbon, scrapbook colors acrylic paint, scrapbook dye, tag and woven label: Making Memories
Other: Balsa wood, plastic heart, ribbon, shipping tags and tulle

HOW TO: Dye all tags and Artisan Label until desired color is achieved and set
aside to dry. With the fold on left, open card and cut a 2¾ x 3¾-inch flap out
of the front flap with a craft knife. Paint square Eyelet Charm, heart brads and
middle sections and edges of Decorative Brads. When dry, place section of
Defined Clear over painted square and trim to fit. Cut a piece of tulle to fit over
flap and adhere. Place square, Woven Label, Decorative Brads and small dyed tag
along left side of the flap. Zigzag stitch the right side of the flap closed. Stick
Artisan Label to balsa wood, trim wood to shape and place plastic heart in the
center. Glue wood to one side of a hinge and adhere the other side behind the
flap. Stamp edges of card with a decorative image. Insert small scraps of folded
ribbon between card flaps and secure with a small amount of adhesive. Stitch
front and back flaps of card together so that card is closed. Print message on small
dyed shipping tag and tie to a larger dyed tag. Wrap ribbon around both tags and
secure with a painted brad. Tuck into top of flap. TIME: 40 MINUTES

HAPPY EASTER BOX
by julie turner

CARD

Artisan labels and scrapbook colors acrylic paint: Making Memories
Computer font: Bernhard Modern by WordPerfect
Other: Candy, jewelry box and twill tape

HOW TO: With a foam brush, paint the outside and inside of a jewelry box using complementary colors. Paint a second coat if necessary. Adhere a large round Artisan Label to the middle of the lid and punch a hole in the center. Print or stamp greeting on a length of twill tape. Thread one end of the twill tape through the hole in the lid and knot on top. Attach the other end to the bottom inside of the box with a small Artisan Label. Use label to write a message if desired. Fill the box with candy, carefully fold twill tape into the box and close.

TIME: 15 MINUTES

ENVELOPE

Artisan label and scrapbook colors acrylic paint: Making Memories
Other: Padded envelope

HOW TO: Paint the envelope using a foam brush. Paint a second coat if necessary. Allow to dry and apply Artisan Label to the front for addressing.

TIME: 5 MINUTES

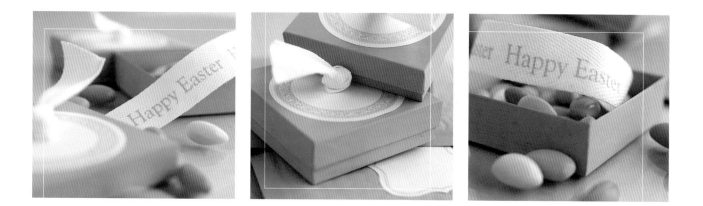

MOTHER
by robin johnson

Beads: DMC
Blossoms, classic small card base and insert, defined, fabric pocket, fabric tag, ribbon, stitches and woven label: Making Memories
Poem: "A Mother's Love" by Sarah Malin
Stamping inks: Colorbox
Other: Lace

HOW TO: Age card and insert by rubbing a stamp pad randomly over surfaces and ink edges of card base. Trim cardstock in a complementary color to the same size as the card and adhere to the inside. Adhere fabric pocket to fabric tag and add lace and letters cut from Defined sticker. Create two flowers by layering two Blossoms together and stitching a bead through the center, knotting on the back of the tag. Glue ribbon to tag for stems and add cross stitches to top left and bottom right corners. Attach embellished tag to the center front of the card. Print and handwrite the words of a poem onto cardstock and cut into strips. Adhere to the insert and add stitches to edges. Place Woven Label below poem and adhere insert to inside flap.

TIME: 25 MINUTES

MOM
by loni stevens

Cardstock tag, cosmopolitan embellishment paper, defined, label holder, latch card base, mini brads and ribbon: Making Memories
Computer font: American Typewriter Light
Other: Button and embroidery floss

HOW TO: Using a craft knife, cut a window out of the front flap of card that measures $3\frac{3}{8}$ x 2 inches. Trim a piece of double-sided paper to fit the back of the front flap, cut out the latch slot and adhere so that pattern shows through the opening. Trim a Defined sticker and a $\frac{3}{8}$-inch strip of patterned paper to fit just below the window and adhere. Create flower petals out of ribbon and glue to bottom right corner of window. Knot embroidery floss through a button and adhere to the center of the flower. Place Defined sticker and Cardstock Tag on the latch and stitch two lines on the end. Trim a piece of paper to fit the larger inside flap of the card and secure by stitching around the perimeter. Print message onto cardstock, cut into a small strip, adhere and attach a label holder over the top. TIME: 35 MINUTES

1. of great worth 2. beloved; cherished

mom

M O t H E R

Mother's Day Cards

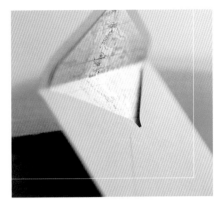
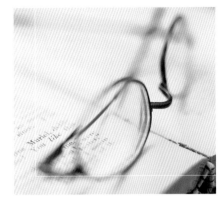

THE BEST DAD IN THE WORLD
by mellette berezoski

CARD
Charmed phrase, scrapbook colors
acrylic paint and washer word: Making Memories
Paper: Bazzill and Design Originals
Other: Negative strip

HOW TO: Cut a piece of cardstock to 5½ x 8½ inches and fold in half to create card. Cut a piece of coordinating cardstock to 3¾ x 4¼ inches and patterned paper to 4¾ x 2¾ inches and layer on front flap. Place a small photo on a negative strip and attach over paper layers. Rub paint into metal pieces, wipe away excess and attach to top left and bottom right corners. Trim a piece of light cardstock and attach inside for writing message.

TIME: 20 MINUTES

ENVELOPE
Paper: Design Originals

HOW TO: Unfold a standard invitation envelope to use as a template. Place over coordinating cardstock, trace, cut, fold and adhere. Trace opening flap onto patterned paper, trim ⅜ inch from the edges and adhere to inside of envelope.

TIME: 10 MINUTES

HAPPY FATHER'S DAY
by loni stevens

Cardstock tag, jump ring, leather frame and mini brads: Making Memories
Computer fonts: American Typewriter Light downloaded from the Internet
and Century by Microsoft Word
Dried fern: Nature's Pressed
Paper: Design Originals
Other: Button, corduroy fabric, jute and transparency

HOW TO: Trim cardstock to 9¼ x 6½ inches and fold in half to create card. Print greeting onto front flap slightly below center. Open card and double stitch around edges of flap. Cut three ½-inch strips of coordinating cardstock, line up just above printed text, trim to fit width of card and adhere. Place brads on ends to secure. Cut a small square of patterned paper and adhere in the middle of the strips. Add dried fern on top and cover with a small piece of transparency. Tie a strand of jute around the bottom right edge of a Leather Frame and dangle a Cardstock Tag from the jute with a jump ring. Stitch a button to a small square of corduroy and sew to bottom right corner of card. Trim a piece of cardstock in the same color as the card to fit the back of the front flap. Attach to hide the stitching and fasteners when card is opened. Cut a ⅞-inch strip of patterned paper and attach on the right side of the inside flap. Print message or poem onto cardstock and stitch inside, slightly overlapping paper border. TIME: 30 MINUTES

Father's Day Cards

HAPPY FATHER'S DAY!

dad

the best dad in the world

Winter Holidays

CHAPTER

Spreading Cheer

Counting Down

Keeping In Touch

...ring Highlights From...

sending love · feeling festive · yearly tradition · spreading cheer · holiday greetings · happy meetings · sharing highlights from the year · keeping in touch · wishing joy and happiness · sending light · topping gifts · hoping for gifts · counting down · remembering the old · ringing in the new

May all your greetings of the season be merry and bright.

CELEBRATE
by kris stanger

Artisan label, defined clear, jump rings, latch card base, ribbon, rub-ons mini, scrapbook colors acrylic paint and tag: Making Memories
Other: Magnets

HOW TO: Using a craft knife, cut a square from front flap of card. Adhere photo inside so that it appears as desired when card is closed. Seal card closed with adhesive and cut off the latch band. Place Defined Clear sticker across the bottom of the card so that it slightly overlaps the photo. Tie ribbon around card gift-wrap style, running it through and knotting it to cover the latch slot. Cut a small tag shape from cardstock and paint surface. When dry, apply rub-ons and punch hole in the top. Dangle a square tag and the painted tag from the ribbon knot with jump rings. Run an Artisan Label through printer to add greeting and apply it and magnets to the back of card.

TIME: 15 MINUTES

CHRISTMAS 2003
by lynne montgomery

Alphabet stamps: PSX Design
Cardstock, eyelet charm, eyelets, jump ring, magnetic date stamp and shaped clip: Making Memories
Computer fonts: CK Corral by Creating Keepsakes and Times New Roman by Microsoft Word
File folder: Autumn Leaves
Photography: Jamie A. Harper
Stamping ink: Staz On by Tsukineko
Other: Jute, old book paper, ribbon, rubber bands and washer

HOW TO: Cut two pieces of cardstock to 6 x 4¼ inches and 5¾ x 4 inches. Scrape and ink edges of smaller piece and adhere at an angle onto first piece. Cut a wide strip of old book paper, attach it diagonally over the mat and add photo. Add a Shaped Clip to the top left corner and a washer with jute tied through to the middle of the right edge. Adhere embellished mat to the inside of file folder. Print message onto cardstock, round corners and ink edges. Cut two rubber bands and stamp greeting along both lengths. Join ends with eyelets and slide around card. Loop a jump ring through eyelet and add Eyelet Charm and ribbon. Stamp family name in the tab.

TIME: 30 MINUTES

JOY, BELIEVE, NOEL
by maggie holmes

Charmed words, fabric swatch, patterned cardstock, ribbon and scrapbook colors acrylic paint: Making Memories
Stamping ink: Ranger Industries

93

HOW TO: Trim cardstock to 10 x 7 inches and fold to create card. Cut a 2⅝ x 7-inch piece of patterned cardstock, ink edges and adhere solid-side up. Stitch around edges. Cut a 4¼ x 3-inch piece of fabric, slightly fray edges, adhere over first strip and zigzag stitch down the right and left sides. Cut another piece of patterned cardstock to 3¼ x 4 inches, ink edges and attach pattern-side up. Stitch around edges. Punch three small holes in patterned block 2 inches in from the edge. Tie three coordinating strips of ribbon through, knotting over the holes. Rub paint onto Charmed Words and, when dry, attach over ribbon. Edge card with two colors of paint. TIME: 15 MINUTES

JOY
by jennifer jensen

Book binding tape, cardstock tag, eyelet charm, mini brads, rub-ons and
scrapbook colors acrylic paint: Making Memories
Paper: Bazzill
Ribbon: Bucilla
Rickrack: Wright's
Other: Chipboard, elastic, velvet holly leaf

HOW TO: Cut a piece of thin chipboard and two colors of cardstock to 8 x 4 inches.
Lay one color of cardstock on top of chipboard and fold a piece of Book Binding
Tape along the top edges to connect the pieces. Adhere rickrack where the tape
meets the paper to cover the seam. Cut three 1⅜-inch squares out of chipboard
and paint. Apply one letter from rub-ons onto each square, center under rickrack
border and adhere. Snip the prongs off two brads and glue where corners meet.
Tie several strands of ribbon to elastic and adhere velvet holly leaf. Place one brad
on each end of the elastic and secure through the back of the card ¼ inch up
from the bottom. Attach so that elastic will be a secure closure to card. Inside,
adhere photo to chipboard. Cut a window out of the second piece of cardstock to
the desired size. Paint Eyelet Charm, edge Cardstock Tag and layer together with a
strip of ribbon in the top left corner of the cardstock. Attach with a brad. Adhere
mat and apply rub-on to photo. Wrap elastic around front, mark where it rests
on either side and cut a small notch out of all three layers. TIME: 30 MINUTES

JOY TO THE WORLD
by erin terrell

Cardstock, charmed, jump ring, latch card base,
ribbon and rub-ons: Making Memories
Threads: Me & My Big Ideas

HOW TO: Apply rub-ons across top of
front flap and on latch of card. Add
handwriting and a woven greeting
under rub-on. Tie a small strip of ribbon around the latch slot and dangle a
charm from a jump ring. Cut a 5-inch
square of cardstock, adhere to inside
and trim to fit if necessary. Adhere a
strip of ribbon down the right side,
lining up edges. Tie and knot two
strips of coordinating ribbon around
the top. TIME: 10 MINUTES

94

JOY To The World
peace on earth

Merry Christmas

JOY

Christmas Cards

Hanukkah Cards

CONGRATS!
by lilac chang

Blossoms, charmed plaque mini, foam stamps, mini brad, rub-ons mini and scrapbook colors acrylic paint: Making Memories
Paper: Bazzill
Other: Vellum and vellum envelope

HOW TO: Cut a piece of 12 x 12-inch paper into four 3 x 12-inch strips. Discard one strip. Fold remaining three strips in half and in half again to create four 3-inch squares on each strip. Attach all three strips together, overlapping end squares of strips—card should have 10 squares. Fold accordion style and use acrylic paint and foam stamps to stamp decorative images and greeting across squares. Paint a vellum envelope and Charmed Plaque Mini and, when dry, attach to end square. Apply rub-on below letter on first square. Fold card and wrap a strip of 1¼-inch vellum around, stapling in the back to close. Layer two Blossoms, attach to vellum with a brad and add decorative stamp. Slide over folded card to hold together. TIME: 25 MINUTES

MAZEL TOV
by erin terrell

Cardstock tag, charmed plaques mini, double-dipped cardstock, eyelet, jump ring, ribbon and safety pin: Making Memories
Computer fonts: AL Eyewitness, AL Highlight, Hannibal Lecter and Tubby downloaded from twopeasinabucket.com

HOW TO: Trim cardstock to 3¾ x 5¼ inches and cut top corners to create a tag shape. Print greeting onto the lighter side of Double-Dipped cardstock, trim to 1¾ inches and mat with darker side. Trim edges to fit the width of the tag and attach to top of card. Add ½-inch strip of darker color below text block and attach three Charmed Plaques Mini on top of the strip. Cut a ⅝-inch strip of cardstock, mat with the darker side and adhere along bottom of tag. Cut a strip of ribbon and attach to the top middle of tag with a safety pin to create the tab. Print remainder of greeting onto a Cardstock Tag, set an eyelet through the hole and dangle from the safety pin with a jump ring. TIME: 15 MINUTES

HI THERE
by maggie holmes

Charm: Westrim Crafts
Defined, jump ring, ribbon, safety pin, staples, upright
slot card base and woven label: Making Memories
Stamping ink: Ranger Industries
Other: Silk flower

HOW TO: Cut cardstock in desired color
to 3¼ x 8½ inches to create insert.
Ink all edges of card and insert. Ink
edges of three Defined stickers and
adhere to insert, lining up edges.
Staple silk flower onto bottom right
corner of insert, ink edges of Woven
Label and place it in the center. Tie
ribbon around slot, knotting on the
left side. Dangle charm from safety
pin with a jump ring and secure pin
through knot. TIME: 10 MINUTES

HAPPY
by mellette berezoski

Charmed plaque mini, defined clear,
ribbon and scrapbook colors acrylic paint:
Making Memories
Paper: Chatterbox and K&Company

HOW TO: Paint grooves and border
of Charmed Plaque Mini and set aside
to dry. Trim cardstock to 6 x 12 inches
and fold to create a square card. Trim
a slightly darker piece of cardstock to
6 x 4¼ inches and, with the fold on
top, adhere to bottom of front flap.
Wrap ribbon around the flap to cover
the seam, joining the ends on the front
of the card. Place Defined Clear sticker
on patterned paper, trimming edges
if necessary. Mat with a coordinating
piece of patterned paper and center
over ribbon, covering ends. Attach
painted plaque to bottom right corner.

TIME: 20 MINUTES

HAPPINESS
by kris stanger

Blossom, label holder, magnetic stamp,
mini brads, ribbon and upright slot card
base and insert: Making Memories
Computer font: Perpetua

HOW TO: Print quote onto insert and
add ornament stamp under text. Slide
through slot, wrap and adhere ribbon
around bottom edge and attach insert
to base. Tie ribbon around top edge,
place label holder over printed word
and Blossom in bottom right corner
of slot and secure all embellishments
with brads. TIME: 15 MINUTES

Phrases, Tips & Templates

APPENDIX A

writer's block · needing inspiration · can't find the right phrase · searching for ideas · throwing a party · creating cards together · preparing for a party · ready to create · how to get started? · making it sincere · saying the right words · postal guidelines · purchasing postage · preparing postage · tools to have on hand · supplies for making fabulous greetings

A helpful, handy guide for finding phrases and tips.

birthday

Let's party!

Look who's turning (age)!

Fun, friends, food

Join us

Calling all party animals

Time to party

Surprise! It's a party

Come to a party

Please come

Let's eat cake

Come on over

You're invited

Celebrate with us!

It's official. She's/He's (age)!

Party on

It's party time!

Happy birthday

Celebrate

Make a wish

Over the hill

You're (age)!

You say it's your birthday…

Call the fire department!

Another year older, another year wiser

It's your day

Hip hip hooray! It's your birthday.

Hope this day is as special as you are.

You're only as old as you think you are.

Birthday wishes

Have your cake and eat it too.

Happy birthday to you

Live it up

It's a beautiful day

Celebrate you

Here's to you

Happy cake and candles day

A friendly birthday wish

It's your birthday again?

Celebrate in style

Birthdays look good on you

Act your shoe size, not your age

So many candles, so little breath

May all your wishes come true

A gift for you

friendship

Hello

Hi there!

You'll always be my best friend-you
    know too much

Best friends forever

Hello, friend

A friend is someone who knows all about you
    and loves you anyway.

Nothing can come between true friends

What would I do without you?

So glad we're friends

Precious and few, loyal and true

You're the best

If friends were flowers, I'd pick you

A friend is there when everyone else walks away

Friendship is a gift

I knew you could do it!

Sending you smiles

You're the best

Believe in yourself

You're absolutely fabulous

Cheer up

You go, girl!

Thinking of you

You're in my thoughts

You've been on my mind

Where have you been?

What's up?

Missing you

Life's not the same without you

I miss you

Wish you were here

Can't wait to see you again

Let's get together

Let's talk

Call me

I have a heavy heart when we're apart

Where has the time gone?

It's been way too long

See you soon

wedding

Let's shower the bride-to-be

Showering you with gifts

Something special for the bride

It's a shower

Here comes the bride

Please come

Save the date

You're invited

Uniting in marriage

Going to the chapel and we're
    going to get married

Request the honor of your presence
    at their marriage

Together with their families invite you to
    join in the celebration of their marriage

Invite you to share their joy

Invite you to their wedding ceremony

Request the pleasure of your company
    at the marriage of

Are delighted to announce the marriage
    of their children

Invite you to share their joy as they
    exchange marriage vows

Cordially invite you to celebrate the marriage of

We hope you will be able to join us
    on our wedding day

Come share our joy

Celebrate with us

Invite you to share our love and friendship
    as we unite in marriage

We're tying the knot

In holy matrimony

Join us for a celebration of love

On this day

I thee wed

Husband and wife

And the two shall become one

Wedded bliss

Now and forever

Happy are those who love and
    cherish one another

Love, honor, cherish

From this day on…

One heart, one love

For the happy couple

Happily ever after

To have and to hold

A day to remember

114

Just married

As one

Old, new, borrowed, blue

A new life together

Eternal love

On your wedding day

Always and forever

A time of celebration, a celebration of love

Best wishes

Hands joined in marriage, hearts joined in love

Beaming, beautiful, blushing bride

She said "yes" and he wrapped
    love around her finger

A perfect union

Together forever, starting right now

love

Have I told you lately? I love you.

With all my heart

I'm all yours

My heart belongs to you

Now, forever, always

You are my everything

So glad you're mine

Sweetheart

You had me at "hello"

The object of my affection

Forever love

Love of a lifetime

I adore you

Truly, madly, deeply

Head over heels

Kiss me, you fool

I believe in us

True love

I got you, babe

I can't live without you

Need you, want you, love you

So happy together

Time stands still when I'm with you

Hey, hottie

Just the two of us

Everlasting love

Always on my mind, always in my heart

You hold the key to my heart

I'm smitten

Crazy for you

Lovestruck

That's amore!

J'taime

Kiss

You have a secret admirer

Love notes

You take my breath away

If you leave me, can I come too?

A perfect match

To my dream guy/gal

Devotion

Hopelessly devoted to you

Side by side

To life, to love, to us

How sweet it is

I love being loved by you

Our love story

All my love, all for you

Sweet on you

We're made for each other

I thank God for lending me you

How do I love thee? Let me count the ways.

Love birds

You complete me

Together is the best place to be

There is no me without you

I can't spell "us" with you.

My one and only

Soul mates

You're everything that means anything to me

Happy anniversary

Still crazy after all these years

A lifetime of memories

I've fallen for you-all over again

Falling in love again

Together in love

Years of wedded bliss

To my better half

Comfy, cozy together

We have so much to remember

Quiet conversations, shared dreams,
    warm memories

baby

Let's shower the mommy-to-be

A shower of love for your baby

Just for baby

It's a boy/girl!

Our house has grown by two feet

She's/He's here!

Special delivery

Fresh from heaven

Our little angel

Our little prince

A precious gift from God

Love at first sight

And baby makes three

First comes love, then comes marriage, then
    comes baby in a baby carriage

Created with love, carried with hope and
    welcomed with joy

Let me introduce myself

A star is born

Our little miracle

Living proof that angels do exist

10 fingers, 10 toes, 1 sweet baby

Welcome, baby!

Welcome, little one!

Heaven sent

Sugar, spice, everything nice

Snakes, snails, puppy dog tails

Tiny fingers, tiny toes, tiny ears, tiny nose

Angel baby

The sweetest thing

Congratulations on your new arrival

Sweet baby

Bundle of joy

Small, soft and sweet

A precious new life to love

We can't wait to meet you

Tiny new baby, great big love

Just heard the news

Pure

Love to you and baby too

Baby mine

On angel wings

Embrace innocence

Precious

expressions

Hooray!

Way to go

Congrats

Congratulations

You did it!

So proud of you

You rock

Consider this a pat on the back

Nice job

Outstanding performance

Great work

Well done

You're awesome

115

Way to go

High five!

Bravo

Here's to you

Wow!

Amazing

You're the bomb!

Gracias, merci, grazie, danke, thanks!

A million thanks

Thanks a bunch

Thanks just doesn't seem like enough

What can I say?

How can I thank you enough?

Thanks for everything

You're the best

I couldn't have done it without you

Hey, thanks

Many thanks

With appreciation

With heartfelt thanks

You made my day

Just a note

Do I need a reason to write?

Just because we're friends

Couldn't wait to say "hi"

sympathy

Thinking of you at this difficult time

With deepest sympathy

Our thoughts and prayers are with you

May your memories be a comfort

Thinking of you in your sorrow

So sorry for your loss

May you find comfort in the love of others

Feel better

Get well soon

Will chicken soup help?

Heard you're under the weather

Take care of yourself

Heard you caught a bug

Cheer up

You'll get through this

Strength, courage

You'll make it

Hang in there

You inspire me

Time heals all wounds

This too shall pass

How can I help?

I'm here for you

Lean on me

Sending happy thoughts your way

Wishing you well

You're not alone

To everything there is a season

Sending you sunshine and cheer

May each day seem brighter and
your load feel lighter

I believe in you

holidays

Sealed with a kiss

Hugs and kisses

Smack!

Be mine, valentine

You + Me = Love

One is good. But two is better.

My heart to yours

XOXO

Roses are red, violets are blue

You're the one for me

Romance

True love

I love you now and always

U R Hot

Red hot

My passion, my fire, my desire

Love of my life

I'm in love. With who? With you!

Love like ours lasts forever

Happy heart day

Hoppy Easter

Have an egg-cellent Easter

Spring fever

New beginnings

Happy everything

Easter blessings

Hop on over

Here comes Peter Cottontail

Easter's on its way

A basket full of fun

Home is where your mom is

Flowers have the sun. Children have their mother.

There's nothing gentler than a mother's hand.

If I didn't have you as my mother, I'd choose
you as my friend.

To my angel mother

You're not just my mom. You're my best friend.

So glad you're my dad

My dad. My hero.

A good dad is hard to find. But the couch is a
good place to start looking.

Any man can be a father, but it takes someone
special to be a dad.

You da man

A father's heart stays with his children forever.

winter holidays

Merry Christmas

Happy holidays

Merry and bright

Remember the reason for the season

Cold hands, warm hearts

Jingle all the way

'Tis the season

Warm winter wishes

Season's greetings

Silent night, holy night

Believe

Ho, ho, ho

Love, peace, joy

Let it snow

Noel

Peace on earth

'Twas the night before Christmas

Gifts of the season

Rejoice

Trim the tree

You better not pout

The magic of Christmas

Meet me under the mistletoe

Deck the halls

Winter wonderland

Celebrate the season

No place like home for the holidays

Santa baby

Naughty or nice?

The stockings were hung

To you and yours

Hark! The herald angels sing

Peace, happiness, joy

Happy 12 Days of Christmas

Holiday cheer

Feliz navidad

Here comes Santa Claus

Joyeaux noel

Baby, it's cold outside

Have a cool yule

Flakes are flying

Be merry

The World Awaits

Gather 'round
The warmth of a fire, the love of a family
O Christmas tree
Happy Hanukkah
Shalom
Dreidel, dreidel, dreidel
Festival of lights
Mazel Tov
Shana Tova
Merry menorah
Light the menorah
A joyous Chanukah
Light up with peace

Blessings for happiness and health
Warm Hanukkah wishes
Light the candles of joy
Miracles, peace, togetherness
May the candles shine bright
Joyous Kwanzaa
It's Kwanzaa time!
Unity, self-determination, collective work and
    responsibility, cooperative economics,
    purpose, creativity, faith
Umoja, kujichagulia, ujima, ujamaa, nia,
    kuumba, imani
Light up your heart

A bright wish for a happy Kwanzaa
Joy and togetherness
Have a colorful Kwanzaa
Love, light and warmth
Happy New Year!
To another year of health and happiness
Out with the old, in with the new
Cheers!
Raise a glass
A toast
10, 9, 8, 7, 6, 5, 4, 3, 2, 1...Happy New Year!
Remember the past, enjoy the present and live
    for the future
New year cheer
Happy (year) to you!

occasions

Hats off to the grad
Con-grad-ulations!
Watch out world-here you come
Wishing you success
Follow your dreams
The future looks bright
Good luck
When one chapter ends, another begins
You're going places, grad
Dressed for success
The world awaits
Knew you could do it
The dream believed is the dream achieved
Today belongs to you
We've moved
We're on the move
Come visit
Our new address
Don't forget us
We've found a new nest
Where we've ended up
We moved-come see where
Come help warm the house
Help us make our new house a home
Our son/daughter is being called to the Torah
Congrats on your bar/bat mitzvah!
On your bar/bat mitzvah
It's your special day
Mazel tov!
May the wisdom of the Torah guide and
    inspire you throughout your life.

117

Hosting a Card Party

Now that you've seen how to make some stunning invitations, make some of your own to throw a card party. It's the perfect way to set aside a dedicated time for creating beautiful cards and spending quality time with girlfriends. Everyone will leave the party with good memories and a ready supply of cards to have on hand to use throughout the year. There are several ways to organize, set up and execute a card party. Choose the format that best fits the skill level, interests and availability of your guests and it's sure to be a raging success. Of course, a good chocolate soufflé will do the trick too.

THE PERFECT
PREASSEMBLED PACKET

SKILL LEVEL: Beginner

PARTY PREPARATION: Design and assemble packets

LENGTH OF PARTY: 3 to 4 hours

DESCRIPTION: Alone or with a co-host, decide on the number and design of cards, assemble all supplies needed and create packets for each guest to create one complete set. Display several finished cards and consider teaching step-by-step so they know what they're working toward.

WHY IT'S GREAT: Guests feel involved in creating cards, it's a great way to introduce friends to cardmaking and it's cost effective to purchase multiples of the same products.

HINT: This can get expensive, so try sharing the cost with your guests. Tally up the cost to create one set of cards, set a price and collect money either with RSVP or the night of the party. Just let them know up front so it's not a surprise when they arrive.

THE GREAT EXCHANGE

SKILL LEVEL: All levels, but best to invite a group with similar abilities and experience

PARTY PREPARATION: Complete cards

LENGTH OF PARTY: 1 hour

DESCRIPTION: Prior to the party, each guest duplicates enough cards of the same design to exchange with the other guests. At the event, the exchanges are made and everyone goes home with a stack of unique cards. Either assign a holiday or subject beforehand or choose a theme so that there are a variety of greetings.

WHY IT'S GREAT: Doesn't require a lengthy time commitment, guests can share their original designs with others and the gathering is more of a social event with lots of ooohing and aaahing.

HINT: Send invitations out early and get firm RSVPs as soon as possible. You want to allow enough time for guests to design and complete cards and you need to communicate the final count to them well before the date of the party.

THE FREE FOR ALL

SKILL LEVEL: Intermediate to Advanced

PARTY PREPARATION: Set up tables and snacks

LENGTH OF PARTY: 1 to 12 hours, depending on how many cards your guests decide to create and how long you'll let them stay.

DESCRIPTION: This party is just like a crop with one exception: No scrapbooking allowed! Let it be known that this is a cards-only crop and let everyone loose.

WHY IT'S GREAT: People can come and go as they please, there is no real structure and it's the set up that allows for the most creative exploration.

HINT: Have a few ideas books around to help inspire your guests while they are designing one-of-a-kind creations.

POSTAL REGULATIONS

The United States Postal Service website provides helpful details and guidelines regarding postage requirements, purchasing postage and preparing postage to ensure accurate, timely delivery. Below are some of these tips. If you need further information or assistance, visit the website at www.usps.com or call 1-800-ASK-USPS. For those outside the United States, contact the postal service in your region for guidelines and regulations.

The postal service classifies the shape of your mailpiece by its dimensions. Since most cards will qualify as letters, check minimum and maximum sizes at www.usps.com/send/preparemailandpackages/measuringtips.htm. For other classifications, visit the website.

Sometimes a mailpiece requires additional postage because it is an unusual size or shape that makes it difficult to process on mail sorting machines. Check with your local postmaster to ensure that you are paying correct postage on your pieces. The following are examples of mail that require extra postage, known as a "nonmachinable surcharge":

Parcel Post
· Parcels less than 6 inches long, .25 inch thick or 3 inches high
· Parcels weighing less than 6 ounces
· Tubes and rolls

First-Class Mail Envelopes
· Square envelopes
· Envelopes on which the address is written parallel to the shorter edge

Purchasing Postage
Stamps are available in many denominations and designs and are available for purchase at post offices, ATMs, grocery and retail stores, banks, by phone at 1-800-STAMP-24 or online at www.usps.com.

Preparing Postage
When sending cards through the mail, careful preparation using guidelines provided by the post office will ensure accurate and timely delivery. A few tips from the website:
· Send cards in standard white, manila or recycled paper envelopes. If items need extra protection, send in bubble-lined, padded or waterproof envelopes.
· Do not use cord, string or twine outside of envelopes as they can get caught in mail-processing equipment.
· Print the delivery and return addresses on the same side of the envelope. The addresses or address labels should be written or placed parallel to the longest side.
· Return address should be placed in the upper left corner.
· Provide a return address so that your mailpiece will be returned to you if it is undeliverable.
· Use the correct spelling of cities, correct abbreviations of states and correct ZIP Codes. Check www.usps.com or call 1-800-ASK-USPS if you need help.

Handwritten notes and cards have been around for hundreds of years. And even in this day of e-mail and voicemail, they're surviving. Making certain that your cards communicate just the right message is easy when you keep these tips in mind:

· Turn speech into script-phrase your message just as you would speak it in face-to-face conversation.
· Spell the recipient's name correctly.
· Find a comfortable place to write.
· Use a good pen that is appropriate for the paper you're writing on.
· Keep all your writing supplies together in one spot or gather them into a container or basket.
· Practice writing your note several times on scratch paper so that your beautifully handcrafted card isn't riddled with cross-outs, misspellings and mistakes.
· Include the date, salutation, text, windup phrase, closing and signature in your correspondence. Limit yourself to one postscript and one small phrase on the back of the envelope if needed.
· Be prompt, generous, specific, succinct and personal.

For further information about writing and creating meaningful cards, check out:

The Art of the Handwritten Note: A Guide to Reclaiming Civilized Communication
by Margaret Shepherd

Finding the Right Words: Perfect Phrases to Personalize Your Greeting Cards
by J. Beverly Daniel

Just a Note to Say...: The Perfect Words for Every Occasion
by Florence Isaacs

Suggested Tools and Supplies

The great thing about cards is that you can make them as simple or elaborate as you want. Several tools and supplies are absolutely essential to cardmaking. Others are commonly used and will give you more design flexibility to create truly stunning greetings. Look for Making Memories cardmaking supplies, embellishments and tools at your local scrapbooking store or at national craft chains.

THE BASICS
Cardstock and/or packaged cards
Envelopes
Paper trimmer
Scissors
Adhesive
Pens
Bone folder
Ruler

MAKING IT FABULOUS
Ribbon
Rub-ons
Metal embellishments
Patterned paper
Fabric
Embroidery floss
Woven Labels
Anything else you use in scrapbooking or other crafts-the sky's the limit!

Artists & Author

MELLETTE BEREZOSKI

LILAC CHANG

MAGGIE HOLMES

JENNIFER JENSEN

ROBIN JOHNSON

LYNNE MONTGOMERY

KRIS STANGER

LONI STEVENS

ERIN TERRELL

JULIE TURNER

JENNIFER KOFFORD *author*

be inspired.™